TABLE OF CONTENTS

Page

DEPARTMENT OF THE NAVY
Headquarters United States Marine Corps
Washington, DC 20380-1775

6 September 2005

FOREWORD

Throughout our Nation's history, we have come to the rescue of oppressed peoples. The Marine Corps, as an elite force, has been called upon time and again to defeat the oppressors. While we Marines fight swiftly and aggressively, we also conduct our military operations with respect toward both the liberated people and the vanquished foe. Compliance with the Law of War is not only required under the Uniform Code of Military Justice (UCMJ), but is also absolutely essential to mission accomplishment. Compliance encourages the civilian populace to cooperate with the Marines and turn-in the foe. It also facilitates the surrender of the enemy, by offering humane treatment rather than a continued fight for a lost cause.

Just as importantly, compliance with the Law of War and the quick reporting of war crimes supports our Nation's values and the purpose behind our involvement in any conflict. To extend freedom, democracy, and the rule of law, we must remain true to the Law of War, to include our international law obligations. America is trusted by the world to do the right thing, and so must be the United States Marines. Following the rules, including the rules in warfare, must be a part of our warrior ethos. The application of honor, courage, and commitment in the conduct of military operations means: the honor to comply with the Laws of War, the courage to report all violations, and the commitment to discipline the violators.

Marine Corps Reference Publication (MCRP) 4-11.8B, *War Crimes*, identifies specific actions that violate the Law of War. It describes the responsibility of every Marine, Sailor or civilian serving with or accompanying the Marine Corps to know and report all suspected, alleged or known violations that are defined by Department of Defense Directive (DODD) 5100.77, *DOD Law of War Program*, and Marine Corps Order (MCO) 3300.4, *Marine Corps Law of War Program*. MCRP 4-11.8B provides specific examples of actions taken by members of military organizations that have been considered violations of the Law of War.

The Law of War is detailed, but it is also easy to follow. The basic principles of the Law of War from MCO 3300.4 are taught to every Marine in basic training:

- Marines fight only enemy combatants.
- Marines do not harm enemy soldiers who surrender. Marines disarm enemy soldiers and turn them over to superiors.
- Marines do not torture or kill enemy prisoners of war or detainees.
- Marines collect and care for the wounded, whether friend or foe.
- Marines do not attack medical or religious personnel, facilities or equipment.
- Marines destroy no more than the mission requires.
- Marines treat all civilians humanely.
- Marines do not steal; they respect private property and possessions.
- Marines do their best to prevent violations of the Law of War, and report all violations to their superiors.

Marines will achieve victory on the battlefield in strict compliance with the Law of War. There is nothing in the Law of War that puts Marines' lives or the mission in jeopardy. Compliance facilitates victory and, at the end of every struggle, Marines will know that they conducted themselves in such a manner as to be judged as worthy successors of a long line of Marines that has gone before them.

MCRP 4-11.8B supersedes MCRP 4-11.8B, *War Crimes Investigation*, dated 22 June 1998.

Reviewed and approved this date.

BY DIRECTION OF THE COMMANDANT OF THE MARINE CORPS

J. N. MATTIS
Lieutenant General, U.S. Marine Corps
Deputy Commandant for Combat Development and Integration

Publication Control Number: 144 000046 00

WAR CRIME DEFINED

It has been the historic practice of the Military Services that a member of the United States (US) military who commits an offense that may be regarded as a "war crime" will be charged under a specific article of the Uniform Code of Military Justice (UCMJ). In the case of other persons subject to trial by general courts-martial for violating the law of war (UCMJ, Article 18), the charge shall be "Violation of the Law of War" rather than a specific UCMJ article.

"War crimes" are defined in the War Crimes Act of 1996 (United States Code [USC], Title 18, Section 2441) as "grave breaches" as defined in the Geneva Conventions of 1949 and any Protocol thereto to which the United States is a party; violations of Articles 23, 25, 27, and 28 of the Annex to Hague Convention IV; violations of Common Article 3 of the Geneva Conventions of 1949 and any Protocol thereto to which the United States is a party and deals with a noninternational armed conflict; and violations of provisions of the Protocol on Prohibitions or Restrictions on the Use of Mines, Booby-Traps and Other Devices (Protocol II as amended May, 1996) when the United States is a party to such Protocol and the violation willfully kills or causes serious injury to civilians.

US policy on application of the Law of War is stated in Department of Defense Directive (DODD) 5100.77, *DOD Law of War Program*, and further explained in Chairman of the Joint Chiefs of Staff Instruction (CJCSI) 5810.01B, *Implementation of the DOD Law of War Program*. "The US Armed Forces will comply with the law of war during all armed conflicts and, unless directed by competent authorities, will comply with the principles and spirit of the law of war during all other operations." See appendix A for examples of war crimes.

LAW OF WAR DEFINED

The law of war is "that part of international law that regulates the conduct of armed hostilities. It is often called the law of armed conflict." The law of war encompasses all international law for the conduct of hostilities binding on the United States or its individual citizens, including treaties and international agreements to which the United States is a party, and applicable customary international law. For example, the Geneva Conventions of 1949 resulted in four agreements that protect wounded, sick, and shipwrecked members of armed forces; prisoners of war (POWs); and civilians in times of war. The 1907 Hague Convention No. IV, *Respecting the Laws and Customs of War on Land*, created guidelines for the conduct of hostilities. Important principles, such as military necessity and the prohibition against unnecessary suffering, can be found in Hague IV.

LAW OF WAR POLICY

US law of war obligations are national obligations, binding upon every Soldier, Sailor, Airman or Marine. Department of Defense (DOD) policy per DODD 5100.77 and CJCSI 5810.01B requires that the US Armed Forces comply with the law of war during all armed conflicts, however such conflicts are characterized, and, unless otherwise directed by competent authorities, the US Armed Forces will comply with the principles and spirit of the law of war during all other operations.

CATEGORIES OF WAR CRIMINALS

Both military and civilian personnel may be categorized as war criminals. While war crimes are most often associated with members of the armed forces, civilians have been known to violate the rights of individuals protected by both the Geneva and Hague Conventions. An example of this is when a civilian attacks or abuses an enemy prisoner of war (EPW) such as a downed pilot. In this instance, the civilian has violated the law of war and is guilty of a war crime. The fact that the civilian is not a member of the military will not exempt him from prosecution in an appropriate forum for law of war violations.

TYPES OF VIOLATIONS

A war crime is technically *any* violation of the law of war by *any* person, military or civilian. However, investigators should primarily concern themselves with violations that are serious in nature (e.g., failing to provide POWs recreation and education opportunities would probably not be prosecuted as a war crime) and that have a nexus to armed conflict (e.g., Iraqi civilians looting other Iraqis would probably not be prosecuted as a war crime, though they may be prosecuted in local courts).

The Geneva Conventions define serious violations against protected persons (e.g., POWs, civilians, wounded, sick and shipwrecked) during international armed conflict as "grave breaches." Grave breaches can include, but are not limited to, the following:

- Willful killing.
- Torture or inhumane treatment.
- Biological experiments.
- Willfully causing great suffering or serious injury.

- Taking hostages.
- Extensive destruction and appropriation of property not justified by military necessity.
- Compelling a protected person to serve in enemy armed forces.
- Willful deprivation of right to a fair and regular trial.
- Unlawful deportation, transfer or unlawful confinement.

Other law of war violations are called simple breaches. Simple breaches include, but are not limited to, the following:

- Using poison or other forbidden arms or ammunition.
- Treacherous request for quarter.
- Maltreatment of dead bodies.
- Firing on undefended localities without military significance.
- Abuse of or firing on flag of truce.
- Misuse of Red Cross/crescent emblem.
- Use of civilian clothing by troops to conceal military character during battle.
- Improper use of privileged buildings for military purposes.
- Poisoning wells or streams.
- Pillage or purposeless destruction.
- Compelling POWs to perform prohibited labor.
- Killing without trial spies or others who have committed hostile acts.
- Compelling civilians to perform prohibited labor.
- Violation of surrender terms.

The designation of a violation of the law of war as a grave or simple breach is a term of art and is not intended to reflect the gravity of the violation or the appropriate disciplinary forum. Parties to the Geneva Conventions must take measures to suppress all war crimes. Furthermore, with respect to grave breaches, parties must enact legislation to provide effective penalties and to search for and try persons suspected of committing or ordering a grave breach, regardless of nationality. The US Government meets this requirement through the UCMJ, and the USC, Title 18, Section 2441, *War Crimes Act of 1996.*

JURISDICTION, STATUTE OF LIMITATIONS, AND PUNISHMENT

War crimes can be tried anywhere, any time. There is universal jurisdiction, and no statute of limitations exists with respect to war crimes.

Court-martial

Members of the US Armed Forces can be court-martialed under specific UCMJ articles (e.g., Article 128 [Assault], Article 118 [Murder], Article 121 [Larceny]) and can be punished accordingly. The UCMJ, Article 18, also authorizes the military to try by general court-martial *anyone* subject to trial by a military tribunal for law of war violations and to adjudge any punishment permitted by the law of war. The law of war does not specify particular punishments; however, punishment must be proportionate to the gravity of the offense.

Federal Court

The War Crimes Act grants federal courts jurisdiction over any person inside or outside the United States for war crimes where a US national or Armed Forces member is accused or is a victim. If the crime results in death to the victim, punishment can include up to life imprisonment or death.

International Tribunal

War crimes may be prosecuted at an international tribunal that is created by allies (e.g., Nuremberg and Tokyo) or created by a United Nations (UN) Security Council Resolution (e.g., former Yugoslavia and Rwanda). Punishment is as authorized by the creating entity.

Military Commissions during Occupation

In occupied areas, courts of the military government can exercise military jurisdiction over individuals, other than members of the occupying forces. Such courts preside in occupied territory and exercise jurisdiction on a territorial basis. The penal laws and punishment of the occupied territory generally remain in force.

Military Commissions under President of the US Order

The President's Military Order of 13 November 2001 authorizes military commissions at any time and place to try non-US al Qaida, international terrorists (e.g., actors, aiders, abettors, conspirators of acts against the United States) and their harborers. Punishment includes life imprisonment or death.

International Criminal Court

The International Criminal Court (ICC) can prosecute war crimes referred by a state party, the UN Security Council or the independent prosecutor. The United States is not a party to the ICC; however, nonparty nationals can be prosecuted with the consent of the suspect's nation or consent of the nation where the crime was committed. Punishment includes up to life imprisonment.

TRAINING AND LEADERSHIP

Marines are less likely to commit war crimes when they are trained in the law of war, understand that anyone who commits violations is a criminal and will be prosecuted, and realize that compliance benefits mission accomplishment. Law of war compliance not only prevents our most valuable asset (personnel) from being jeopardized, but also may—

- Increase public and international support of the US military.
- Encourage reciprocal treatment by the enemy with respect to US servicemembers who are held captive.
- Help end the conflict more quickly by minimizing hostilities.

Marine Corps Order (MCO) 3300.4, *Marine Corps Law of War Program*, and Marine Administrative Message 182/04, *Marine Corps Law of War Program*, set forth the law of war training requirements for the Marine Corps. Commanders must become familiar with these requirements and ensure their subordinates are trained accordingly. Commanders must stress the importance of law of war compliance and impose on subordinates an expectation that they will not commit violations. An explicit stigma against such activity, coupled with a vigilant awareness of factors that contribute to the commission of war crimes, can minimize the potential for subordinates to engage in such activity.

Historically, a number of factors have been found to lead to the commission of war crimes. Effective training and leadership operate to eliminate some of these factors as follows:

- High friendly losses.
- High turnover rate in the chain of command.
- Dehumanization of the enemy or use of derogatory names or epithets.

- Poorly trained or inexperienced troops.
- Poor small unit discipline standards.
- The lack of a clearly defined enemy.
- Unclear orders.
- High frustration level among the troops.

COMMAND RESPONSIBILITY

Commanders are responsible for training their subordinates on the law of war and for reporting and investigating reportable incidents, as well as preventing and correcting violations. Additionally, under the UCMJ, commanders are legally responsible for violations committed by subordinates if any one of the following three circumstances apply:

- The commander ordered the commission of the act.
- The commander knew of the act, either before or during its commission, and did nothing to prevent or stop it.
- The commander should have known "through reports received by him or through other means, that troops or other persons subject to his control [were] about to commit or [had] committed a war crime and he fail[ed] to take the necessary and reasonable steps to insure compliance with the law of war or to punish violators thereof." (Field Manual 27-10, *The Law of Land Warfare.*)

Note: In international tribunals, commanders have been held personally responsible for violations committed by subordinates if the commander ordered the commission of the act or if the commander knew or should have known of the act either before or during its commission and did nothing to prevent or stop it.

INCIDENT REPORTING

A "reportable incident" is a possible, suspected or alleged violation of the law of war. Per DODD 5100.77; CJCS1 5810.01B; and Secretary of the Navy Instruction (SECNAVINST) 3300.1A, *Law of Armed Conflict (Law of War) Program to Insure Compliance by the Naval Establishment*; or their current editions, it is DOD, joint, and Department of the Navy policy that:

- The law of war obligations of the United States are observed and enforced by DOD components.
- All "reportable incidents" committed by or against members of, or persons serving with or accompanying the US Armed Forces, must be promptly reported, thoroughly investigated, and, where appropriate, remedied by corrective action.
- All "reportable incidents" committed by or against allied military or civilian personnel or by or against other persons during a conflict, to which the United States is not a party, will be reported through appropriate command channels for ultimate transmission to appropriate US agencies, allied governments or other appropriate authorities. Once it has been determined that US persons are not involved in a reportable incident, an additional US investigation shall be continued only at the discretion of the appropriate combatant commander. On-scene commanders shall ensure that measures are taken to preserve evidence of reportable incidents pending turnover to US, allied or other appropriate authorities.

Consistent with DODD 5100.77 and SECNAVINST 3300.1A or their current editions, all Marines, Sailors, and civilian personnel serving with or accompanying the Marine Corps who have knowledge of, or receive a report of an apparent "reportable incident," will comply with the requirements set out below. As soon as practical:

- Inform the immediate commander of the matter.
- Make the matter known to an officer (normally in the chain of command) senior to the immediate commander if the member has an honest and reasonable belief that the immediate commander is, or may be, involved in violating or concealing a violation of the law of war.
- In circumstances making other means of reporting impractical, report the matter to a chaplain, judge advocate or military police investigator who shall then report the matter as directed in MCO 3300.4.

INITIAL REPORT

The commander of any unit that obtains information about a reportable incident will:

- Take immediate action to mitigate or correct the harm.
- Report the matter promptly through command channels, to higher authority.
- As soon as practical, report the matter to the nearest military police investigator.
- If practical, secure the scene of the possible law of war violation so that evidence may be preserved and collected.

Higher authorities receiving an initial report will:

- Report the incident by the most expeditious means to the responsible combatant commander. Absent other applicable directives, commanders will normally report "reportable incidents" by means of an operational report-3 (MCO 5740.2F,

OPREP-3SIR: Serious Incident Reports). The Commandant of the Marine Corps (CMC) (Deputy Commandant for Plans, Policies, and Operations, Operations Division/Security Division; Inspector General of the Marine Corps; and Staff Judge Advocate to CMC, International and Operational Law Branch) will be designated as information addressees on all reports of "reportable incidents."

- Request a formal investigation by the cognizant military investigation authority.

NOTORIETY OF WAR CRIMES

Due to the notoriety associated with war crimes, it is especially important for an investigator to perform a diligent investigation. While having a Marine identified as a suspect in a war crimes investigation brings discredit upon the United States Marine Corps (USMC), a deficient investigation would only add to the adverse publicity. It is far better if a thorough investigation is conducted and the appropriate disciplinary action carried out than for an alleged war crime to be perceived as being covered up. Inadequate investigations could lead to accusations of a cover up of the alleged war crime, which then could seriously undermine public support for military operations.

SPECIAL CONSIDERATIONS

The investigation of an alleged war crime should be treated like any other criminal investigation. However, three specific considerations should be taken into account:

- The need for interpreters.

- An armed guard force to assure personal security and protection of witnesses and evidence.
- The Rome Statute of the ICC.

The Rome Statute of the ICC is a treaty that went into effect 1 July 2002 without US support. The ICC claims jurisdiction over genocide, crimes against humanity, war crimes, and crimes of aggression. The ICC poses a concern to Marines deploying to ICC-party nations, as ICC parties may attempt to turn Marines over to the ICC for prosecution. To counter these novel provisions, the United States is negotiating Article 98 Agreements, under which countries agree not to turn over US personnel without US consent. Furthermore, commands should not turn custody of Marines over to foreign officials without approval from appropriate higher authority.

CONTACTS

If you have any questions concerning war crimes, contact the Security and Law Enforcement Branch at Headquarters, USMC. The mailing address and telephone numbers are as follows:

COMMANDANT OF THE MARINE CORPS (PS)
Security and Law Enforcement Branch
Security Division
Headquarters, US Marine Corps
Washington, DC 20380-1775
Commercial: (703) 614-4177, 614-1068
DSN: 224-4177, 224-1068

Appendix A
Identification of War Crimes

Note: Some of the examples are followed by a list of UCMJ articles that may be charged in addition to Articles 92 and 134.

The willful killing, torture or inhumane treatment of individuals protected by the Geneva Conventions.

Individuals protected from willful killing, torture or inhumane treatment include—

- EPWs.
- Medical and religious personnel.
- Sick, wounded, and shipwrecked combatants (also includes crews from disabled aircraft).
- Civilian internees, refugees, and other civilians under a military organization's control.

Inhumane treatment includes willfully causing great suffering or serious injury to body or health. Inhumane treatment may be as serious as beatings, but it may also take the form of systematically ignoring or neglecting the needs (shelter, clothing, food, water, and medical attention) of detainees (EPWs and interned civilians) who are entitled to certain protections under the Geneva Conventions.

An example of inhumane treatment is ordering an EPW to turn over to his captor his rations, boots, winter coat, first-aid kit, and shelter when the EPW still needs these items.

Article 93	Cruelty and Maltreatment
Article 118	Murder
Article 119	Manslaughter
Article 120	Rape and Carnal Knowledge
Article 122	Robbery
Article 124	Maiming
Article 128	Assault
Article 134	General Article (indecent assault, negligent homicide)

Note: Article 134 addresses offenses that involve disorders and neglects to the prejudice of good order and discipline in the Armed Forces, bring discredit upon the Armed Forces, or involve noncapital crimes or offenses that violate Federal law.

The unlawful and wanton destruction or illegal taking (confiscation or stealing) of property (e.g., medical, religious, educational, scientific, and cultural property) that is protected by the Geneva and Hague Conventions.

This law of war violation also includes private property that has no military value (e.g., looting private homes is prohibited) and the personal property of EPWs. EPWs must be allowed to retain possession of their personal property, protective gear, valuables, and money, subject to valid security concerns, such as protection from theft and violence. Personal items must not be taken unless properly receipted for and recorded as required by Geneva Conventions Relative to the Treatment of Prisoners of War (GPW), 12 August 1949, Article 18. USC, Title 10, Section 2579, *War Booty: Procedures for Handling and Retaining Battlefield*

Objects, and Section 7216, *Collection, Preservation and Display of Captured Flags,* set forth procedures for the handling and retaining of battlefield objects and flags and mandate that all enemy material and flags captured or found abandoned shall be turned in to appropriate personnel, except in accordance with regulations issued by the Secretary of Defense.

Article 99	Misbehavior Before the Enemy
Article 103	Captured or Abandoned Property
Article 109	Property Other than Military Property of US—Waste, Spoilage, or Destruction
Article 121	Larceny and Wrongful Appropriation
Article 122	Robbery

Forcing an EPW or alien civilian to serve in your own forces or to act as a guide for these forces.

Willfully depriving an EPW or a civilian who is in custody of the due process right to a fair and regular trial for allegedly committed offenses.

This rule prohibits, among other things, summary executions in the field for alleged misconduct or spying.

Unlawful deportation, transfer or confinement of civilians under the control of a military force or government.

For example, when hostilities broke out in Kuwait, US or allied civilians in Kuwait were illegally transferred to Iraq and confined there by the Iraqi government.

Taking of civilians as hostages.

Using poison, bacteriological agents, and other weapons determined by higher authority to be illegal because they are calculated to cause unnecessary suffering.

Article 124   Maiming

The mistreatment, abuse, neglect or collective punishment of EPWs (including religious and medical personnel) or civilians in the custody of US Armed Forces.

Mistreatment can include acts of intimidation, insults or ridicule toward an EPW. This type of misconduct may take the form of a Marine posing for a photograph of himself holding a gun to the head of a blindfolded EPW.

Article 93   Cruelty and Maltreatment
Article 128   Assault

Refusing quarter (the opportunity to surrender) unless bad faith is reasonably suspected.

Marines do not have to stop in the middle of a firefight to accept someone's surrender, nor are they obligated to put themselves at risk to accept surrender. However, Marines may not refuse to accept a surrender if they have the means to safely accept the surrender.

> **Giving a treacherous (false) request for quarter or misuse of a flag of truce (white flag).**

This example of a war crime covers the situation in which a Marine attempts to trick his enemy into believing that he wishes to surrender or negotiate a truce to take advantage of his enemy.

> **Misusing the Red Cross insignia or other protective emblems.**

In most Moslem nations, the protective emblem for medical service personnel and equipment is the Red Crescent. In addition to the Red Cross or Red Crescent, there are also protective emblems for religious and cultural buildings. Buildings and ships holding EPWs or civilian internees are required to display the emblems PW (which identifies them as POW camps) or IC (which identifies them as an internment camps) to indicate that they should not be targeted.

Placing a red cross or any other protective emblem on a building to trick the enemy into believing that the facility is a hospital, POW camp or internment camp is against the law of war.

> **Firing on a flag of truce (white flag).**

> **Violating surrender or truce terms.**

Attacking the enemy without justification during a truce or a cessation in hostilities is against the law of war.

| Pillaging or purposeless destruction of property. |

Article 99	Misbehavior Before the Enemy (quitting place of duty to plunder or pillage)
Article 103	Captured or Abandoned Property (dealing in, looting, or pillaging)
Article 109	Property Other than Military Property of US—Waste, Spoilage, or Destruction
Article 121	Larceny and Wrongful Appropriation

| Looting or theft. |

Theft and looting also includes the taking of personal property from EPWs or civilians for personal enrichment.

Article 103	Captured or Abandoned Property (dealing in, looting, or pillaging)
Article 109	Property Other than Military Property of US—Waste, Spoilage, or Destruction
Article 121	Larceny and Wrongful Appropriation
Article 122	Robbery

| **Forcing an EPW or civilian to perform prohibited labor.** |

EPWs cannot be used to design or construct items whose primary use is for military gain (e.g., a bridge that would help Marines attack the enemy). Labor that is humiliating, inherently dangerous (e.g., clearing minefields) or a health hazard is prohibited.

Ordering an EPW to assist sick or wounded Marines is not prohibited because the Marines are considered to be noncombatants while they are sick or wounded. EPWs may also be required to perform such labor as—

- Administrative work.
- Installation repair and maintenance.
- Agricultural work.
- Manufacturing and transportation work that serves no military purpose.
- Domestic work.
- Work related to the arts.

| **Transferring an EPW to people (military or civilian) of a country that did not sign the Geneva Conventions.** |

Before transfer to a country that did sign the Conventions, the United States must be satisfied that the receiving country is willing and able to apply the Conventions (GPW, Article 12).

> **Executing or otherwise punishing (without a trial) an individual accused of being a spy or a saboteur.**

> **Article 18   Murder**
> **Article 119   Manslaughter**

> **Attacking an undefended town or a civilian object that has no military significance.**

> **Mutilating corpses.**

The mutilation of corpses (e.g., cutting off ears as a war trophy) is strictly prohibited under the law of war.

> **Executing any form of reprisal against a person protected by the Geneva Conventions.**

People protected by the Geneva Conventions can include, but are not limited to, civilians not engaged in hostilities; an EPW or a sick, wounded or shipwrecked enemy combatant. However, if a civilian (an unprivileged combatant) shoots at Marines while they are patrolling an occupied town, the civilian may be fired on. If the civilian is apprehended, he must be given a trial or hearing before being punished for his actions. If the civilian eludes capture, the Marines may not harm the home or property of the suspected sniper's relatives or friends as a form of reprisal. Similarly, if the identity of the sniper is unknown, the Marines may not institute any sort of collective punishment (e.g., cut off electricity or water in the town) directed at the neighbors of the civilian sniper. Reprisals are not permitted, except with the specific approval of the President or Secretary of Defense.

> **Article 109   Property Other than Military Property of US—Waste, Spoilage, or Destruction**

Placing a bounty or reward for killing an enemy, individual or a member(s) of a particular military organization.

Attacking Red Cross or Red Crescent personnel, vehicles or buildings or the wounded they are assisting.

Placing EPWs or civilians in unsafe or unhealthy locations.

Placing an EPW or a civilian near legitimate military targets (i.e., using them as human shields).

Using an EPW or civilian as a human shield is a violation of the law because—

- If the target is attacked, the EPW or civilian may be harmed.
- If the attackers refrain from targeting the legitimate military target for fear of harming noncombatants, the Marines who placed the noncombatants in harm's way have taken an unlawful military advantage.

> **Article 93   Cruelty and Maltreatment**
> **Article 118   Murder**
> **Article 119   Manslaughter**
> **Article 134   General Article (negligent homicide)**

Forbidding alien civilians, especially women and children, from departing an enemy nation once hostilities have commenced.

Draft age male civilians may be interned by their enemy if it is suspected that they may enter the armed forces of their nation once they return to their homeland. However, women and children should not be stopped from fleeing an enemy nation and returning to their homeland.

Failing to notify an EPW's government of the fact the individual has been captured and keeping interned alien civilians incommunicado.

Confiscating food, water, medicine, etc., from detained civilians due to the fact that they are enemy aliens or are subjects of the country being occupied.

Article 103	Captured or Abandoned Property (looting or pillaging)
Article 121	Larceny and Wrongful Appropriation
Article 122	Robbery

Forcing civilians to commingle with troops in an attempt to have the enemy refrain from attacking the combined group.

Article 93   Cruelty and Maltreatment

Encouraging or forcing refugees to place themselves in the path of an attacking enemy to hinder the enemy's advance.

Article 118   Murder
Article 119   Manslaughter
Article 134   General Article (negligent homicide)

Failing to search out, collect, make provision for the safety of, or to care for survivors of sunken ships or boats when the military situation permits.

Failing to care for members of enemy or friendly armed forces in the field, when the military situation permits, who are disabled by sickness or wounds or who have dropped their weapons and surrendered.

Attacking individual civilians who are not actively engaged in direct hostilities against friendly forces or the civilian population.

Executing indiscriminate attacks on the civilian population or civilian property is unlawful, knowing the attack will cause—

- Loss of life or injury to civilians.
- Damage to civilian property that would be excessive or disproportionate in relation to the concrete and direct military advantage anticipated, and cause death or serious injury to body or health.

Article 118	Murder
Article 119	Manslaughter
Article 128	Assault
Article 134	General Article (negligent homicide)

Poisoning wells, streams or other water sources.

Pretending to be wounded.

Pretending to be wounded is unlawful if it is part of a plan to—

- Take advantage of the enemy's obligation not to attack wounded combatants.
- Attack the enemy when his guard is down. Indicating to an enemy that you are unable, due to your wounds, to continue to fight has the same effect as indicating (by raising your hands over your head or waving a white flag) a desire to surrender.

Forcing an EPW or civilian to collect wounded fellow Marines from the battlefield during the battle.

Executing physical or mental coercion toward an EPW or a civilian while in custody to induce him to provide information.

For example, threatening to throw someone out of a helicopter unless he provides information.

Article 93   Cruelty and Maltreatment

Appendix B
Glossary

CJCSI .... Chairman of the Joint Chiefs
of Staff instruction

CMC...............................Commandant of the Marine Corps

DOD.. Department of Defense

DODD .... Department of Defense directive

EPW .... enemy prisoner of war

GPW........... Geneva Conventions Relative to the Treatment
of Prisoners of War

ICC...International Criminal Court

MCO ....Marine Corps order

MCRP ....Marine Corps reference publication

POW... prisoner of war

SECNAVINST................. Secretary of the Navy instruction

UCMJ................................ Uniform Code of Military Justice

UN.. United Nations

US .... United States

USC...United States Code

USMC .... United States Marine Corps

Appendix C
References

United States Code (USC)

Title 10, Sec. 2579   War Booty: Procedures for Handling
                        and Retaining Battlefield Objects

Title 10, Sec. 7216   Collection, Preservation and Display of
                        Captured Flags

Title 18, Sec. 2441   War Crimes Act of 1996

Department of Defense Directive (DODD)

5100.77   DOD Law of War Program

Chairman of the Joint Chiefs of Staff Instruction (CJCSI)

5810.01B   Implementation of the DOD Law of War
                        Program

Secretary of the Navy Instruction (SECNAVINST)

3300.1A   Law of Armed Conflict (Law of War)
                        Program to Insure Compliance by
                        the Naval Establishment

Marine Corps Orders (MCO)

3300.4   Marine Corps Law of War Program

5740.2F   OPREP-3SIR: Serious Incident Reports

Marine Administrative Message (MARADMIN)

182/04   Marine Corps Law of War Program

Army Field Manual (FM)

27-10   The Law of Land Warfare

Miscellaneous

1907 Hague Convention No. IV, Respecting the Laws and Customs of War on Land